Siciliano on

CAME TO MY RESCUE

MUSIC BY

Dylan Thomas, Joel Davies, Marty Sampson

ARRANGED FOR SOLO PIANO BY

Ken Medema

worship BRIDGES

Siciliano on
Came to My Rescue

Music by Dylan Thomas,
Joel Davies, Marty Sampson
Arranged by Ken Medema

25
31
37
f
43
49

56
61
67
73
dim.
mp
79

85
91
97
103
molto rit.
109
a tempo

114
120
126
132
138
f

144
150
156
162
168

173
rubato
dim.
p
179
185
191
197

203
cresc.
209
215
p
221
cresc.
227
dim.
rit.

233
pp
239
molto rit.
245
a tempo
mel. lower note
pp
251
mp
257

263
269
276
f
282
288

294
301
307
312
rit.
a tempo
dim.
p
319